Say It Right in English 2

Say What You Mean, Mean What You Say

ネイティブが気になる日本人の英語 2

Mark Thompson

Toshihiro Tanioka

EIHŌSHA

テキストの音声は、弊社 HP
http://www.eihosha.co.jp/の
「テキスト音声ダウンロード」
のバナーからダウンロードでき
ます。

はしがき

　フリーダイアル、リュック、セレブ、アポ、パワハラ、ガッツポーズ、メジャー、サイン、コンセント、マイナンバーに CA、OB …。また「準備中」「使用中」「閉鎖中」等の意味で使われている 'CLOSE'。正しい英語のようで誤用英語か和製英語のような。また、短縮されて元の語（句）が不明になったような。我々、日本人が日常生活で見聞きし、自らも使用するこの類の語（句）や表現には枚挙に暇がありません。

　本書は 'Say It Right in English（ネイティブが気になる日本人の英語）' の続編です。本書も英語学習者がより一層、正しい英語を学ぼうという意識を持ち、それを深化していただきたいという思いから著わしました。換言すると、学生に英語の授業内外で、英語の誤用、和製英語、日本語を文字通り英訳した不自然な英語表現等を改め、自然で正しい英語を学び、かつ、表現する意識を育んでいただきたいということです。

　こうした趣旨を基本に、本書で扱える対象も限定的ですが、新たにいくつかの特徴を持たせました。

　まず、本文（passage）は、平易な英文で読みやすくし冗長にならないように留意しました。次に、その内容は、語法に問題のある英語表現、短縮して意味不明になり混乱等を招きかねない英語表現、一単語の使用方法で違いが出る英語表現等に着眼してみました。更には、日本語式発音がもたらす問題、変化し続ける表現等にも着目し、改めて自然で正しい英語学習の必要性への意識醸成に努めました。加えて、英語として文法上の問題は無いが、場面によっては不自然、相手には不快となる表現等も取り上げ、その問題点を指摘してより良いコミュニケーションがはかれるように努めました。そうした中でも、話題の語を含む正しい英文例を示しその理解度、実用度を高める工夫もしています。

　コミュニケーションの手段の基本は言葉です。口語であれ文語であれ、その基本は、語（句）や文章です。外国語でコミュニケーションが上手く正しくはかられるためには、その外国語を学習する者も指導する者も、その言葉の正しい意味、語法、文法、そして発言する TPO にも留意することが肝要です。2020 年の東京オリンピック、パラリンピック、2025 年の大阪万博の開催時は言うに及ばず、今後も日本では様々な国際イベントの開催が続き、観光客も含め多くの外国人の訪日が予想され英語でコミュニケーションをとる機会も増えることでしょう。逆に日本人が海外に出掛けて英語でやり取りをする場合もあります。英語だけがコミュニケーション手段ではありませんが、英語でコミュニケーションをはかる場合に正しい自然な英語を使うことは、日本（人）の印象を良くする一助にもなるでしょう。

　こうした事を主眼にしつつ、このテキストには、以下のような構成上の特徴を持たせています。

・半期完結用の全 15 課の無駄の無い構成。また、毎回扱うトピックを独立させ、学生は、毎授業、新鮮な気持ちで取り組めます。最終ユニットは Review ＋ として本文、内容の理解チェックも。

・各ユニットは 4 技能（読、書、聴、話）のバランスの取れた構成。1 ユニットは 1 演習（90 分）で完結。目安は、「本文読解理解 40 分」「聴解 15 分」「Writing Exercise（書）25 分」「Dialog（ミニ英会話）5 分」。
授業形態によっては全てをカバーせず一部割愛も可能です。

・本文の読解・理解（Reading）には、その指針となる質問（Q、原則 2 つ）と語（句）のヒント。辞書で単語を引く手間が軽減され、本文の内容把握がよりスムーズにできるだけでなく予習もしやすい。

・英検と TOEIC の問題形式を模した聴解練習（Listening）。まず、本文 Passage の内容に関して質問文以外はテキストに記載した選択肢からの解答形式（英検）。また各ユニットには Additional Listening Practice として TOEIC 形式の Question & Response か Short Conversations の問題を追加。

・文法の項目に沿った英作（Writing）。語順を問う基礎問題（3 問）と、難度を上げて語彙力、文法力、表現・作文力を問う自由英作（3 問）の 2 部構成で英作の苦手な学生と基礎問題で物足りない学生の両方に対応。

・Dialog（ミニ英会話 /Speaking）。すぐに使える海外旅行時の表現と日常生活に使える表現。書き取り練習を通して音声からも身につけられる工夫。全て易しい単語の短文で覚えやすい。

・各ユニットの最後には One Step Forward を追加。正しい英語表現力を更に高めます。

　本書が学生の正しい英語を学ぼうという意識向上と英語教育の改善、成果に幾分でも寄与できれば、本書を上梓した甲斐があると考えます。
　こうした私共の意を汲み、本書の出版に賛同してくださった英宝社社長の佐々木　元氏と、編集、校正段階で大変お世話になった同社編集部の下村　幸一氏らに心から謝意を表します。

2019 年（令和元年）晩秋

著　者

Contents

Say It Right in English 2
Say What You Mean, Mean What You Say

ネイティブが気になる日本人の英語 2

Unit 1　Closed

I　Vocabulary Checking

A群の英単語の日本語訳をB群より選びその記号を［　］に記入しなさい。

A群

1 customer　［　］　　2 engagement　［　］　　3 depart　［　］

4 apart　　　［　］　　5 ad　　　　　　［　］　　6 exam　　［　］

B群

a 離れて　　**b** 出発する　　**c** 試験　　**d** 婚約　　**e** 客　　**f** 広告

II　Reading

☆ **Before Reading Passage** （Q［質問］を念頭に Passage［本文］を読んでみましょう）

　Q1 日常生活で時々、目にする 'Close'（準備中、使用中、閉鎖中等）は正しい英語？ spell（スペル）は？

　Q2 日本語のアイス、アパート、デパート等は正しい英語の意味で使われているでしょうか。

☆ **Words & Phrases** （単語、語句のヒント）

1 witness ～を見かける　　2 typical 典型的な　　3 construction 建設、工事　　4 noun 名詞

5 erroneous 誤った　　6 fake 偽の　　7 abbreviate ～を省略する　　8 automobile 車

☆ **Passage**

In their daily life in Japan, native English speakers often [1]witness incorrect usage in English. One of the [2]typical examples is '**Close**' on the door of a store. The shop owner should put a sign '**Closed**' to tell customers that the store is not open but is closed. The same sign can be seen at a checkout lane in a store, on the door of a meeting room, or on a road under [3]construction. Use the word spelling not **spell**, which as a [4]noun means magic or a short period of time. "The witch put the princess under a **spell**, and she fell asleep for ten years." "He stopped for a rest, and after a short **spell**, he started to work again."

In food and drinks, too, we can see similar [5]erroneous Japanese English. *Ice coffee* and *ice tea* should be iced coffee and iced tea respectively. Say hamburger or hamburger steak for *hambâgu*, which sounds like a city name in Germany, Hamburg. Say 'omelet on rice' for *omu-raisu*. A 'decorated cake' is a better expression for *decoration cake*, which sounds like a [6]fake cake. In saying **ice**, make it clear whether it is frozen water or ice cream. Also, use 'soft serve ice cream' for *soft cream* or *soft ice cream*. Similarly, 'tea with milk' for *milk tea*.

Also, native English speakers often do not understand shortened or [7]abbreviated forms of English expressions widely used in Japan. They never say **apart** for apartment or apartment building and **depart** for department store. **Apart** means to be separated by distance or time and **depart** means to leave. Never say *apo* for appointment. Say celebrity for *serebu* and accelerator for *akuseru* in an [8]automobile. Also, use the phrases 'engagement ring' for *engage ring*, 'hair dryer' for **dryer** and 'cloak room' in a hotel for **cloak** The word **dryer** means a machine to dry clothes and the **cloak** a sleeveless coat.

Shortened or abbreviated forms are acceptable when they are correctly understood and widely used. **TV** for television, **ad** for advertisement, **exam** for examination, the **flu** for influenza and **ID** for identification are typical examples. So are **PS** for postscript, **PC** for personal computer, **ASAP** for as soon as possible, and **PK** for penalty kick in a soccer match.

III Listening Comprehension

Listen to the CD and choose the correct answer about the passage.

1 A Yes, it is widely seen on a road under construction.

   B Customers can tell the store is not open.

   C We can see one at a checkout lane in a supermarket.

2 A It can mean either frozen water or ice cream.

   B It should be used as 'iced cream' as iced tea.

   C **Ice tea** is a shortened form of **iced tea**.

3 A It means to fully spell a word without shortening any word.

   B It can mean a certain period of time.

   C Yes, it means **spelling** as a verb.

4 A Dryer is the shortened form of hair dryer.

   B The word depart has come to mean department store recently.

   C The word exam is widely used as the shortened form of the word examination.

Additional Listening Practice 1

Listen to the CD and choose the best answer or a statement as a response.

1 A B C

2 A B C

Ⅳ Writing Exercise 1 （be 動詞）

Exercise 1 ［　　］内の語（句）を並べ替え日本文にあう英文を書いてみましょう。

（注：文頭の文字サイズと句読点は、要適宜対応）

1 新しい我が家は、その駅からは近くない。

［near, our, is, the station, house, not, new］

→＿＿＿＿＿＿＿＿＿＿＿＿＿＿＿＿＿＿＿＿＿＿＿＿＿

2 私は医師で、姉は看護師です。

［am, a nurse, is, elder, and, doctor, I, sister, a, my］

→＿＿＿＿＿＿＿＿＿＿＿＿＿＿＿＿＿＿＿＿＿＿＿＿＿

3 10 年前、この市にはホテルは二つしかなかった。

［only, ago, this, were, in, ten years, city, hotels, there, two］

→＿＿＿＿＿＿＿＿＿＿＿＿＿＿＿＿＿＿＿＿＿＿＿＿＿

Exercise 2 次の各日本文にあう英文を書いてみましょう。

1 ここからそのバス停まで距離はどれくらいありますか。

［ヒント：距離が（ある）☞ far］

→＿＿＿＿＿＿＿＿＿＿＿＿＿＿＿＿＿＿＿＿＿＿＿＿＿

＿＿＿＿＿＿＿＿＿＿＿＿＿＿＿＿＿＿＿＿＿＿＿＿＿

2 「これは君の手袋ですか。」「いいえ、僕のではないです。」

→＿＿＿＿＿＿＿＿＿＿＿＿＿＿＿＿＿＿＿＿＿＿＿＿＿

＿＿＿＿＿＿＿＿＿＿＿＿＿＿＿＿＿＿＿＿＿＿＿＿＿

3 先々週、私の両親が休暇で京都にいた時、運悪く、お天気は良くなかった。

→＿＿＿＿＿＿＿＿＿＿＿＿＿＿＿＿＿＿＿＿＿＿＿＿＿

＿＿＿＿＿＿＿＿＿＿＿＿＿＿＿＿＿＿＿＿＿＿＿＿＿

V　Dialog（ミニ英会話 1）

Listen to the CD and fill in the blanks.（CD を聴き空白部分を書き取りましょう）

Immigration（空港の入管）　［A: An immigration officer（入管係官）　B: A traveler］

A: May I see your passport?

B: _____ _____ _____.

A: What's the purpose of your visit?

B: Sightseeing. _____ _____ _____

_____.

A: How long are you going to stay?

B: _____ _____ _____.

A: Fine. _____ _____ _____.

◇関連表現◇　上記の下線の文と併せて覚えましょう。

　　　1　何か申告する物はありますか。いいえ、何もありません。

　　　　Do you have anything to declare?　No, nothing.

　　　2　こちらにはビジネス / 出張で来ています。

　　　　I'm here on business.

One Step Forward 1

次は英語では短縮化、または省略され一般化した表現です。何のことでしょう。

① mayo　　② info　　③ FAQ　　④ DIY

答 ☞ 次頁。

One Step Forward 1 の答

①　mayo ＝ mayonnaise（マヨネーズ）

②　info ＝ information（情報）

③　FAQ ＝ frequently asked questions

（よくある質問）

④　DIY＝do it yourself（日曜大工）

Unit 2　Excuse Us

I　Vocabulary Checking

A群の英単語の日本語訳をB群より選びその記号を［　　］に記入しなさい。

A群

1 meal　　　［　］　　2 client　　　　［　］　　3 polite　［　］

4 profession　［　］　　5 expression　［　］　　6 hobby　［　］

B群

a 職業　　**b** 食べ物、料理　　**c** 趣味　　**d** 表現　　**e** 客、顧客　　**f** 丁寧な

II　Reading

☆ **Before Reading Passage**（Q［質問］を念頭に passage［本文］を読んでみましょう）

Q1 Excuse me. と Excuse us. の使い分けは？

Q2 相手の名前、趣味等を尋ねる際の望ましい英語表現は？

Q3 男女同権・平等は、どういう形で英語に表れているでしょうか。

☆ **Words & Phrases**（単語、語句のヒント）

1 colleague 同僚　　2 co-worker ＝ colleague　　　3 the former 前者　　4 the latter 後者

5 rude 失礼な　　6 provided that ～ ～という前提で　　7 gender 性　　8 replace 取ってかわる

☆ **Passage**

What would you say in English in the following situations? Suppose you and your friend are in an elevator with some others in front of you, and you two want to get off the elevator when it stops at your floor. You might say '**Excuse me**'. How about the case that you and your partner or a ¹colleague are having lunch with some guests or clients? Now you and your partner or ²co-worker have to leave the table for a while in the middle of the meal. Do you say '**Excuse me**', in this situation, too? Acceptable and understandable though it is, it would be more suitable and natural here in both cases to say '**Excuse us**,' since there are two of you leaving the elevator or getting up from the meal. Also, it would be better to say "I'm afraid I（we）have to be going now," than simply saying "I（we）have to leave." ³The former sounds like you would rather stay but **HAVE TO** leave for some reason while ⁴the latter sounds like you do not want to stay there any longer.

When you ask someone you meet for the first time his or her name, it would be better and polite to say, "I am Kenji Sato. May I have your name?" Or' "Do you mind if I ask your name?" Depending on the situation, it can be a little [5]rude to say, "What's your name?" Some native English speakers might think, "What do you want to know my name for? You'd better say your name, first!" Similarly, instead of saying "What is your hobby?", it would be better to say, "What do you like to do in your free time?" or "Do you have any hobbies?" You may ask the former question [6]provided that the person being asked **DOES** have a hobby.

Be aware of changes in a language. [7]Gender equality has gained more and more understanding. It has been long since **Ms**. has [8]replaced **Miss** and **Mrs**. **Ms**. does not consider whether a woman is married or not. In referring to professions and positions, too, such words as **officer**, **firefighter**, **anchor**, and **chairperson** or simply **chair** have all [8]replaced **policeman**, **fireman**, **anchorman**, and **chairman** respectively. Also, the word **sibling** has become more common for brother and sister. Also, it is better to say **African-Americans** in referring to **blacks**. However, it is acceptable to say **blacks** in some cases such as in comparing racial groups. "Relations between blacks and whites in the region seem good."

Ⅲ Listening Comprehension

Listen to the CD and choose the correct answer about the passage.

1   A   It may sound a little rude to some people.

   B   Yes, it is quite the same as "May I have your name?"

   C   Some native English speakers want to know your name first.

2   A   to ask him or her on a date

   B   to say that you are not busy

   C   to ask how he or she spends their time when not busy

3   A   Excuse me.

   B   How about another cup of coffee?

   C   Yes, you should leave a tip for the waiter serving you.

4   A   An officer means a policeman.

   B   'Blacks' cannot be used for 'African-Americans' any longer.

   C   Ms. came to be used for Miss and Mrs. a long time ago.

Additional Listening Practice 2

Listen to two short conversations and choose the best answers to the questions.

1　A　She'll be dating a Japanese man and she's a little nervous now.

　　B　She will be talking about some manners in Japan.

　　C　She is going to be one of the judges for a speech contest.

　　D　She will attend a seminar to learn Japanese manners.

2　A　He will go to see a doctor.

　　B　He will major in medicine in college.

　　C　He will buy some new headsets for his music player.

　　D　He will buy some medicine for his headache.

IV　Writing Exercise 2（動詞①―現在形）

Exercise 1　［　　　］内の語（句）を並べ替え日本文にあう英文を書いてみましょう。

（注：文頭の文字サイズと句読点は、要適宜対応）

1　私の祖父は毎朝、その公園を散歩します。

[takes, the park, my, a walk, in, morning, grandpa, every]

➜ _____

2　信号が青に変わるまでここにいなさい。

[light, the, blue, until, here, turns, stay]

➜ _____

3　メアリーはトムを信頼していない。というのも、彼はよく嘘をつくからだ。

[lies, Mary, because, often, doesn't, he, trust, Tom]

➜ _____

Exercise 2　次の各日本文にあう英文を書いてみましょう。

1　僕は普段は徒歩で通勤しますが、雨の日にはバスを利用します。

［ヒント：〜を利用する　☞ take］

_____

_____

2　珍しい本を多く所蔵するという理由から、その新しい市立図書館には多くの人が訪れる。　　　　　　［ヒント：珍しい ☞ rare］

_____

_____

3 「ニューヨークからロサンゼルスまで航空運賃はいくらかかりますか。」「旅行する
時期によります。」

_____

_____

V Dialog（ミニ英会話 2）

CD
1-9

Listen to the CD and fill in the blanks.（CD を聴き空白部分を書き取りましょう）

Checking in at a Hotel（ホテルのチェックイン）

[A: A hotel clerk　B: A Japanese traveler]

A: Good evening, sir. _____ _____ _____
_____?

B: Yes, I have a reservation. My name is Kenji Sato.

A: _____ _____ _____ _____
_____again, please?

B: Sato, it's S-A-T-O.

A: Thank you very much. Yes, Mr. Sato. We have your reservation.
Will you fill out this form, please?

B: Sure.（*A few minutes later*）_____ _____
_____.

A: Thank you, sir. _____ _____ _____
_____?

B: With my card.

◇関連表現◇　上記の下線の文と併せて覚えましょう。

　　　1　予約はしていないけど今夜泊まる部屋ありますか。
　　　　I have no reservation, but do you have a room for me tonight?
　　　2　鍵を持たずに部屋を出てしまいました。
　　　　I've locked myself out.
　　　3　エアコンの調子が良くないです。
　　　　The air-conditioner is not working（properly）.

One Step Forward 2

次の日本語にあたる英語表現は何でしょう。

① ライトアップ ② タイムアップ ③ スピードダウン

答 ☞ 次頁。

One Step Forward 2 の答

① ライトアップ　　lightening-up or illumination

② タイムアップ　　The time is up.

③ スピードダウン　reduce the speed or decelerate

Unit 3　A Seed of Misunderstanding

I　Vocabulary Checking

A群の英単語の日本語訳をB群より選びその記号を［　　］に記入しなさい。

　A群

　　1 free 　　　［　］　　2 bachelor ［　］　　3 reception ［　］

　　4 baggage ［　］　　5 missing ［　］　　6 vehicle ［　］

　B群

　　a 受付　　**b** 行方不明　　**c** 乗り物　　**d** 独身　　**e** 自由な、暇な、無料の　　**f** 荷物

II　Reading

☆ **Before Reading Passage**（Q［質問］を念頭に passage［本文］を読んでみましょう）

　Q1 英語で時間を尋ねる時、どんな事に注意すべきでしょうか。

　Q2 'look for a wife' と 'look for my wife'、"Call me a doctor." と "Call me doctor." の各々の違いは？

☆ **Words & Phrases**（単語、語句のヒント）

　1 subtle 微妙な　　　2 confusion 混乱　　　3 misunderstand 〜と誤解する　　4 spouse 奥さん、配偶者

　5 freeway 高速道路　　6 consider 〜とみなす　　7 hesitant ためらって　　8 avoid 〜を避ける

☆ **Passage**

　A ¹subtle difference or error in using words makes a big difference in meaning and may cause ²confusion or unexpected results. You may ask someone near you what time it is. You can say, "Excuse me but do you **have the time**? Be sure that you do not say, "Excuse me but do you **have time**?" The latter means that you are asking the person if he or she is free. He or she may even ³misunderstand that you are asking him or her on a date!

　Suppose you and your ⁴spouse are on a tour bus. You may want to sit **in the front of the bus** but never **in front of the bus**. The latter means that you want to be somewhere **OUTSIDE** the vehicle, probably right before the bus. You can say, "I would like to sit in the front of the bus," though. Also, you can say in a short form, "I would like to sit in front," assuming that the listener understands the reference to a location inside the bus. Similarly, if you say, "I'm looking for **a wife**," it can mean that you are a bachelor and want to find someone to marry. On the other hand, "I'm looking for **my wife**." means that your wife travelling with you maybe got lost or was missing while the tour bus was at a rest stop, not a **service area**, next to the [5]freeway.

You may unfortunately get sick at night in a hotel while travelling in America. You may call the reception desk at the hotel and ask the staff to call you a doctor. You can just say, "Could you please **call me a doctor**?" But if you say, "Could you please **call me doctor**?" instead, it may confuse the staff. It is all right if you are **a doctor** and your name is **Sato**, for example, and you want to be called **Dr. Sato** instead of **Mr. Sato**. The staff might [6]consider it an unusual request in the middle of the night. He may reply by saying, "Yes. **Dr. Sato**. What can we do for you?" Also, make sure that you say when checking out, '**Call me a taxi**,' if you want the hotel staff to call you a taxi to go to the airport. Never say "**Call me taxi**'.

Make no misunderstanding that you do not need to be [7]hesitant to speak out in English being afraid of making errors. But speaking proper English helps to [8]avoid troubles. Have a nice trip.

Ⅲ　Listening Comprehension

CD
1-11

Listen to the CD and choose the correct answer about the passage.

1　A　We may ask someone for a date.
　　B　Yes, we usually watch our steps.
　　C　We may ask someone near us.

2　A　to ask if he or she is free
　　B　to ask what time it is
　　C　to ask what he or she wants to do in their free time

3　A　when your wife gets lost somewhere
　　B　to travel together
　　C　if you are a bachelor

4　A　to ask them to call a doctor
　　B　at the time of checking out
　　C　a taxi to go to the airport

Listen to the CD and choose the best answer or a statement as a response.

1 A B C

2 A B C

Ⅳ Writing Exercise 3（動詞②—過去形 & 未来形）

Exercise 1 ［　　］内の語（句）を並べ替え日本文にあう英文を書いてみましょう。

（注：文頭の文字サイズと句読点は、要適宜対応）

1　昨夜、ボブは彼の両親に手紙を書いた。

［to, night, a letter, Bob, wrote, his parents, last］

➡＿＿＿＿＿＿＿＿＿＿＿＿＿＿＿＿＿＿＿＿＿＿＿＿＿

2　兄が今日、何時に学校から帰宅するか僕は知らない。

［will, today, know, time, from, I, school, my brother, come, don't, home, what］

➡＿＿＿＿＿＿＿＿＿＿＿＿＿＿＿＿＿＿＿＿＿＿＿＿＿

3　僕は風邪を引いたので、今日の午後、病院に行くつもりだ。

［a doctor, and, caught, I, this, see, go, will, a cold, afternoon, to, I］

➡＿＿＿＿＿＿＿＿＿＿＿＿＿＿＿＿＿＿＿＿＿＿＿＿＿

Exercise 2　次の各日本文にあう英文を書いてみましょう。

1　先月、ビルは落馬して右足を折った。

［ヒント：落馬する＝馬から落ちる☞落ちる ☞ fall］

➡＿＿＿＿＿＿＿＿＿＿＿＿＿＿＿＿＿＿＿＿＿＿＿＿＿

＿＿＿＿＿＿＿＿＿＿＿＿＿＿＿＿＿＿＿＿＿＿＿＿＿＿

2　「君はそのニュースを聞いた時、何をしましたか？」「直ぐに両親に電話をしました。」

➡＿＿＿＿＿＿＿＿＿＿＿＿＿＿＿＿＿＿＿＿＿＿＿＿＿

＿＿＿＿＿＿＿＿＿＿＿＿＿＿＿＿＿＿＿＿＿＿＿＿＿＿

3　私の両親が今夕、空港に何時に着くか主人に話すのを忘れた。

➡＿＿＿＿＿＿＿＿＿＿＿＿＿＿＿＿＿＿＿＿＿＿＿＿＿

＿＿＿＿＿＿＿＿＿＿＿＿＿＿＿＿＿＿＿＿＿＿＿＿＿＿

V Dialog（ミニ英会話3）

Listen to the CD and fill in the blanks.（CDを聴き空白部分を書き取りましょう）

At a MacDonald's（マクドナルドで）［A: A shop staff B: A Japanese traveler］

A: Hi. ＿＿＿＿＿＿＿ ＿＿＿＿＿＿＿ ＿＿＿＿＿＿

＿＿＿＿＿＿ ＿＿＿＿＿＿＿?

B: A Big Mac, large French fries, salad, and a diet Coke.

A: What size drink do you want?

B: Large, please.

A: Is that ＿＿＿＿＿＿ ＿＿＿＿＿＿ ＿＿＿＿＿＿

＿＿＿＿＿＿ ＿＿＿＿＿＿?

B: For here.

A: That's $12.75.

B: Here you go.

A: Out of twenty. ＿＿＿＿＿＿ ＿＿＿＿＿＿ ＿＿＿＿＿＿. Have a

nice day.

◇関連表現◇　上記の下線の文と併せて覚えましょう。

　　1　（夕方以降）ごきげんよう。

　　　　Have a nice evening.

　　2　メニューを見せてください。

　　　　May I see the menu?

One Step Forward 3

単語１語の使い方で意味が大きく違う場合があります。次の１、２の英訳でそれぞれ正しいのは？

1 「ご出身はどちらですか。」
　ア　Where do you come from?　イ　Where did you come from?

2 「それについてどう思いますか。」
　ア　What do you feel about it?　イ　What do you think about it?
　ウ　How do you feel about it?　エ　How do you think about it?

答 ☞ 次頁。

One Step Forward 3 の答

1 ア
（イは「どこから来たのですか。（＝ここに来る前はどこにいたのですか。）」

2 イ、ウ 共に正解。

Unit 4　Job Placement

I　Vocabulary Checking

A群の英単語の日本語訳をB群より選びその記号を［　　］に記入しなさい。

A群

1 firm 　　［　　］ 　　2 profession 　　［　　］ 　　3 graduate(s) 　　［　　］

4 outdated 　　［　　］ 　　5 application 　　［　　］ 　　6 interview 　　［　　］

B群

a 応募 　　**b** 会社 　　**c** 面接（試験） 　　**d** 卒業生 　　**e** 時代遅れの 　　**f** 職業

II　Reading

☆ **Before Reading Passage**（Q［質問］を念頭に passage［本文］を読んでみましょう）

Q1 日本語で使う CA（客室乗務員）は正しい英語なのでしょうか。　OB や OG はどうでしょうか。

Q2 学生の就職試験で大事な要素は何でしょう。また、そのために学生はどんな準備をし、また気を遣いますか。

☆ **Words & Phrases**（単語、語句のヒント）

1 job placement 就職 　　2 referred to ～と言う 　　3 gender equality 男女平等

4 (well) versed 良く知る 　　5 fare（事が）上手くいく 　　6 vital factor 非常に重要な要素

7 attire 服装 　　8 asset 人材、財産

☆ **Passage**

One of the popular jobs for Japanese college students is [1]job placement at airlines. Especially, for some female students, working as a staff in the plane cabin is a dream-come-true. While it is usually [2]referred to as **CA**, standing for *cabin attendant* in Japan, the correct English is **flight attendant** or one of the cabin crew. The once widely-used word **stewardess** seems to be outdated now. Likewise, not *grand hostess* but **ground staff** is correct English for the female staffers at or around the airline counters and boarding gates in airports. In both cases we can see [3]gender equality has advanced to this level.

Whatever job or profession it may be, there seem to be some important factors to be successful in achieving job placement. One of the key factors is to get well [4]versed with the company in advance. Many students collect information about a company through its website. Some acquire advice and information in a traditional way from their so-called **OBs** (old boys) or **OGs** (old girls) who graduated from the same college and are currently employed at the workplace. In English, these words are referred to as alumni or simply graduates. **OB** means out of bounds in golf. Besides, neither boys nor girls are usually old.

What counts most, however, is how you [5]fare or perform at the interview. Besides the **resume** which describes motivation for application and skills, your communication skills during the interview can be a [6]vital factor to win job placement at the company. Make your **selling point**, not *sales point*, clear in the interview. Also, making a good impression may depend on proper [7]attire. Male students usually wear a tie and so-called *recruit suit* and a *Y-shirt*, each of which should be a suit and a dress shirt respectively in English.

Once you start your career at the firm, you are expected to be an [8]asset there as an employee. Here you can use similar expressions such as **office worker** or **salaried worker** depending on where you work. However, never say *salaryman* or **OL**, neither of which are correct English.

III Listening Comprehension

CD
1-15

Listen to the CD and choose the correct answer about the passage.

1   A   It is right English but is outdated now.
    B   It is not correct English, but it is widely used to refer to a flight attendant in Japan.
    C   It means staff working at or around the airline counters at airports.

2   A   a suit and a dress shirt
    B   Yes, they usually try to learn about the company in advance.
    C   They try to make their selling points clear.

3   A   salaryman
    B   employee
    C   sales point

4   A   Yes, you are expected to be an asset to the company.
    B   Getting advice or information from graduates is no longer as useful as it used to be.
    C   the performance at the interview as well as the resume

Additional Listening Practice 4

Listen to two short conversations and choose the best answers to the questions.

1 A in a restaurant in the hotel

   B Mr. Sato will be paying in the lobby.

   C in his hotel room

   D Mr. Sato will be having a glass of red wine.

2 A She will go to a nearby coffee shop.

   B She and Cathy will be having a cup of coffee in the living room.

   C She will give Cathy a ride to the nearest train station.

   D She will go to the kitchen.

Ⅳ Writing Exercise 4 （助動詞）

Exercise 1 ［　　］内の語（句）を並べ替え日本文にあう英文を書いてみましょう。

（注：文頭の文字サイズと句読点は、要適宜対応）

1 外は大雪に違いない。

[be, hard, it, outside, must, snowing]

➔ _____

2 君は必ずその仕事ができると私は確信している。

[do, that, you, am, can, sure, the work, I]

➔ _____

3 我々が旅行で留守中、ペット（複数）はどうしようか。

[we, on, do, away, what, our pets, while, our trip, should, we, about, are]

➔ _____

Exercise 2 次の各日本文にあう英文を書いてみましょう。

1 「学生証を見せてもらっていいですか。」「はいどうぞ。」

[ヒント：証 ☞ ID]

➔ _____

_____

2 我々はそのガイドさんを待たねばならなかったので時間通りには出発できなかった。 [ヒント：ガイド ☞ tour guide]

➔ _____

_____

（次頁に続く）

3 直ぐに出発した方がいいよ。そうしないと、東京行きの新幹線に間に合わないよ。

[ヒント：そうしないと☞ or、〜行きの ☞ bound for 〜]

→ _____

_____

V　Dialog（ミニ英会話 4）

CD
1-17

Listen to the CD and fill in the blanks.（CD を聴き空白部分を書き取りましょう）

Getting Lost（道に迷って）　[A: A Japanese traveler　B: A stranger]

A: Excuse me, but _____ _____ _____

_____?

B: Sure, if I can. _____ _____ _____?

A: _____ _____. How can I get to the Hilton Hotel?

B: It's just around that corner. _____ _____

_____ _____.

You can't miss it.

A: Thank you so much.

B: Not at all.

◇関連表現◇　上記の下線の文と併せて覚えましょう。

1 （それは）右手に見えてきます。

You'll see it on your right.

2 （我々は）この地図の何処にいるのでしょうか。

Where are we now on this map?

One Step Forward 4

How Do You Say it in English?　（次の日本語にあたる英単語（句）は何でしょう。）

① フリーター　② ホームヘルパー　③ ノルマ
④ ハードスケジュール　⑤ トリマー

答 ☞ 次頁。

One Step Forward 4 の答

① フリーター　a part-time worker

② ホームヘルパー　a home care worker

③ ノルマ　quota

④ ハードスケジュール　tight schedule

⑤ トリマー　groomer

Unit 5 Harassment

I Vocabulary Checking

A群の英単語の日本語訳をB群より選びその記号を［　　］に記入しなさい。

A群

1 spread　［　　］　　2 superior　［　　］　　3 behavior　［　　］

4 momentum　［　　］　　5 hesitation　［　　］　　6 occur　［　　］

B群

a 上司、上役　　**b** 勢い　　**c** ためらい、躊躇　　**d** 広がる　　**e** 起る　　**f** 行い、振舞い

II Reading

CD
1-18

☆ **Before Reading Passage**（Q［質問］を念頭に passage［本文］を読んでみましょう）

Q1 2017 年、何がありましたか。

Q2 日本で使用されている「ハラスメント」にはどういうものがありますか。英語表現としては正しいのでしょうか。

☆ **Words & Phrases**（単語、語句のヒント）

1 accuse 非難する　　　　2 sexual predators 性的加害者・犯罪者　　3 accusation 非難

4 abuse 悪用　　　　　　5 subordinates 部下　　　　　　　　　　6 bullying いじめ

7 pregnant 妊娠した、身重の　8 discrimination 差別

☆ **Passage**

In the late 2010s, the "# *Me Too Movement*" caught nationwide attention in America. In 2017, actor Alyssa Milano on Twitter [1]accused the famous Hollywood film producer Harvey Weinstein of sexual harassment. Similar sexual harassment cases had often been unreported, but the movement to publicly call out [2]sexual predators gained momentum following her open [3]accusation. It even seems to have spread worldwide. The phrase sexual harassment is correct English and is widely used in Japan, too. But its shortened form **seku-hara** does not make sense to native English speakers.

While the word harassment is used correctly in some cases, in other cases, it is not. The phrase *power harassment* seems to require more time to be understood by native English speakers, let alone its shortened form **pawa-hara**. It refers to a type of harassing behavior or [4]abuse of power by superiors or senior co-workers to their [5]subordinates in workplaces. It also applies to [6]bullying by senior colleagues or members to their juniors in workplaces or organizations. **Workplace harassment** based on status or power differentials may make more sense.

Also in Japan, treating or harassing a [7]pregnant woman unfairly due to her condition occurs in workplaces. Harassment against the woman may continue even after giving birth. In Japan, it is called *maternity harassment* or **mata-hara** in short. The phrase might make sense to some but pregnancy harassment or [8]discrimination may sound more natural to native English speakers.

While in college, you may encounter **academic harassment**. It usually refers to such harassment cases of professors against their students in their academic performance as well as their junior faculty or staff. Like **pawa-hara**, a shortened form **aka-hara** does not make sense in English at all.

Last but not least, asking a woman her so-called *three size* can be sexual harassment. Although it is not rare in Japan to ask women their size and for them to reply them with little hesitation, the *three size*, measurements in proper English, is one of the most improper questions to ask a woman in western cultures.

III Listening Comprehension

CD
1-19

Listen to the CD and choose the correct answer about the passage.

1 A Its shortened form aka-hara makes sense in English.
   B to ask a female student of her measurements
   C harassing students or junior professors or staff by professors

2 A Sexual harassment cases came to be much more widely and openly reported.
   B An American actor made her debut in a Hollywood movie.
   C They produced a movie entitled 'Sexual harassment'.

3 A She never tweets.
   B She had experienced sexually harassment by a movie producer.
   C She visited Japan in 2017 to tell about various sexual harassment cases in America.

4 A Yes, they are.
   B It is not clear from the passage.
   C No, pregnant women in many workplaces there are not fairly treated.

Additional Listening Practice 5

Listen to two short conversations and choose the best answers to the questions.

1　A　B　C

2　A　B　C

Ⅳ　Writing Exercise 5（進行形）

Exercise 1　[　　]内の語（句）を並べ替え日本文にあう英文を書いてみましょう。

（注：文頭の文字サイズと句読点は、要適宜対応）

1　私の母は今、台所で皿洗いをしています。

[in, is, the, my, washing, kitchen, now, the dishes, mother]

→＿＿＿＿＿＿＿＿＿＿＿＿＿＿＿＿＿＿＿＿＿＿＿＿＿

2　トムは車を運転しながらメールを打っていた。

[was, a, he, a car, was, while, texting, Tom, driving, message]

→＿＿＿＿＿＿＿＿＿＿＿＿＿＿＿＿＿＿＿＿＿＿＿＿＿

3　私がベンチで昼食をとっている間、数人の男の子が公園でサッカーをしていました。

Some boys [the park, was, lunch, playing, having, on, were, while, soccer, the bench, in, I]

→ Some boys＿＿＿＿＿＿＿＿＿＿＿＿＿＿＿＿＿＿＿＿＿

Exercise 2　次の各日本文にあう英文を書いてみましょう。

1　「その時、君は、何をしていたのですか。」「二階で自分の部屋の掃除をしていました。」

→＿＿＿＿＿＿＿＿＿＿＿＿＿＿＿＿＿＿＿＿＿＿＿＿＿

＿＿＿＿＿＿＿＿＿＿＿＿＿＿＿＿＿＿＿＿＿＿＿＿＿＿

2　「トムはあそこで何をしているのですか？」「車の鍵を捜しています。」

［ヒント：〜を捜す ☞ look for 〜］

→＿＿＿＿＿＿＿＿＿＿＿＿＿＿＿＿＿＿＿＿＿＿＿＿＿

＿＿＿＿＿＿＿＿＿＿＿＿＿＿＿＿＿＿＿＿＿＿＿＿＿＿

3　「ちょっと待ってくれ。今、靴下を履いている。」「わかった。ロビーで（君を）待ってるよ。」　　　　　　　　　　　　　　［ヒント：〜を履く ☞ put on ］

→＿＿＿＿＿＿＿＿＿＿＿＿＿＿＿＿＿＿＿＿＿＿＿＿＿

＿＿＿＿＿＿＿＿＿＿＿＿＿＿＿＿＿＿＿＿＿＿＿＿＿＿

V Dialog（ミニ英会話 5）

Listen to the CD and fill in the blanks.（CD を聴き空白部分を書き取りましょう）

At a Bank（銀行で）　［A: A clerk　B: A Japanese traveler ］

A: _____ _____ _____ _____?

B: Yes. I want to cash some of my traveler's checks.

A: Certainly. _____ _____ _____ here?

　　How much do you want to cash?

B: Two hundred dollars.

A: _____ _____ _____ _____

　　_____?

B: Five twenties, eight tens and twenty singles, please.

A: All right. Here you go. _____ _____

　　_____ _____.

◇関連表現◇　上記の下線の文と併せて覚えましょう。

　　　　1　小銭もお願いします。

　　　　　　I want some change / coins, too.

　　　　2　こちらに口座を開設したい。

　　　　　　I want to open an account here.

One Step Forward 5

How Do You Say it in English?　（次の日本語にあたる英単語（句）は何でしょう。）

①　ペアルック　　②　コンビ　　③　ミスコン

④　ランニングマシーン（ルームランナー）　　⑤　ドクターストップ

答 ☞ 次頁。

One Step Forward 5 の答

①　ペアルック　twin outfits

②　コンビ　duo, pair

③　ミスコン　beauty contest

④　ランニングマシーン（ルームランナー）　treadmill

⑤　ドクターストップ　doctor's order

Unit 6　Major or Measure

Ⅰ　Vocabulary Checking

A群の英単語の日本語訳をB群より選びその記号を［　　］に記入しなさい。

A群

　1 pronunciation　［　　］　　2 tip　　［　　］　　3 political science　［　　］

　4 repair　　　　　［　　］　　5 sew　［　　］　　6 measure　　　　　　［　　］

B群

　a 政治学　　**b** 発音　　**c** 〜を修理する　　**d** 縫う　　**e** 〜を測定する　　**f** 心付け、ご祝儀

Ⅱ　Reading

☆ **Before Reading Passage**（Q［質問］を念頭に passage［本文］を読んでみましょう）

Q1 日本語式で発音する英語のバイキング、チップ、ミシンは正確に通じているのでしょうか。

Q2 英単語の major と measure の違いは？

☆ **Words & Phrases**（単語、語句のヒント）

1 usage 語法　　　　　　　　2 integrated circuit（ＩＣ）集積回路　　3 adjective 形容詞

4 industry (ies) 産業　　　　5 length 長さ　　　　　　　　　　　6 mixture 混合、混ぜ合わせ

7 suppose 〜と仮定する　　　8 avoid 〜を避ける

注 missing（人、物等が）行方不明、抜けている

　　　　　　　例文 Police are searching for the missing girl. / His name is missing from the list.

☆ **Passage**

In learning a foreign language, correct pronunciation is as important as [1]usage and grammar. Japanese English learners need to heed it in pronouncing such English sounds like 'v' and 'r'. Incorrectly pronounced, it may cause misunderstanding. "Let's go to a *biking* (viking) restaurant for lunch." Most Japanese mean by this to have lunch at a buffet restaurant, namely an all-you-can-eat restaurant. Some native speakers, however, may imagine going to a restaurant *biking*, that is by bicycle!

Most Japanese pronounce the word **tip** as if it were **chip**. **Tip** means an additional amount of money given to someone such as a waiter or a taxi driver for their service while **chip** means a small piece of wood or stone, or a small [2]integrated circuit (IC)

used in computers. Also, Japanese usually do not say **sewing machine** but simply say *mishin*, which is usually pronounced like [注] **missing**.

Likewise, in Japan, the English word **major** is often pronounced like another English word **measure**. It can be confusing to some English speakers because **major** means the main subject you study at a college or to study something as the main subject at a college. "My major is political science." "I am majoring in economics." It is also used as an [3]adjective to mean very large or important. "My car needs major repairs." "Shipbuilding used to be one of the nation's major [4]industries." The word **measure**, on the other hand, means to find the size, [5]length or amount of something. "Let's measure the floor to see if the carpet will fit." Here you need a tape measure, not simply a measure, to find out the length. The word also means to judge the importance or value of something. "It is hard to measure educational success by e-learning."

A [6]mixture of incorrect choice of words and wrong pronunciation makes things worse. [7]Suppose you want to buy a motorcycle but say to an American friend of yours, "I want an *ōtobai*." It may sound to your American friend, "**I ought to buy.**" Your friend may say to you, "Oh, what do you have to buy?" For your further learning, to [8]avoid misunderstanding, it seems better to say **motorcycle** instead of saying **bike** because it means both a bicycle and a motorcycle in English.

III Listening Comprehension

Listen to the CD and choose the correct answer about the passage.

1 A It is given by a waiter to a customer.
   B a small stone used in a computer
   C to a taxi driver

2 A It means to find out how long a thing is.
   B the main subject you study at a college
   C the importance or value of something

3 A It is difficult to enter a college.
   B It means the main subject you study at a college.
   C It is sometimes used for the word measure.

4 A by bicycle   B by motorcycle   C We can hardly tell.

Additional Listening Practice 6

Listen to the CD and choose the best answers to the questions.

1 A by taxi   B by hotel bus

   C by airport limousine   D His friend gave him a ride.

2 A The guest is checking out the Marriot Hotel in Atlanta.

   B The Marriot Hotel has a bus terminal next to it.

   C The guest paid $12.50 for the bus fare from the hotel to the airport.

   D The guest did not make any calls from his room.

Ⅳ　Writing Exercise 6 （受動態・受身）

Exercise 1　［　　］内の語（句）を並べ替え日本文にあう英文を書いてみましょう。

（注：文頭の文字サイズと句読点は、要適宜対応）

1　このかわいい人形はメアリーが作ったのですか。

[made, this, by pretty, Mary, doll, was]

→ _____

2　晴れの日には、我が家から富士山が見える。

[can, on, seen, Mt. Fuji, our, a, from, be, clear, house, day]

→ _____

3　あの角の販売店では、アメリカ車も販売されているよ。

[are, the dealership, corner, cars, on, the, also, American, sold, at]

→ _____

Exercise 2　次の各日本文にあう英文を書いてみましょう。

1　カナダでは、英語とフランス語が話されている。君の国では何語が話されていますか。

→ _____

_____

2　学校へ行く途中で、僕らはにわか雨にあった。

[ヒント：にわか雨 ☞ shower]

→ _____

_____

3　我々は、トムがそのチームのキャプテンに選ばれなかったという知らせに驚いている。

→ _____

_____

V   Dialog （ミニ英会話 6）

Listen to the CD and fill in the blanks. （CD を聴き空白部分を書き取りましょう）

At a Post Office   [A: A post office clerk   B: A Japanese traveler]

A: May I help you?

B: I _____ _____ _____ _____
_____ to Japan by airmail.

A: Let me weigh it first.

B: _____ _____ _____ _____.

A: Forty-five dollars.

B: _____ _____ _____ _____
_____?

A: About a week.

B: Fine. And give me ten twenty-five cent stamps, please.

A: That's forty-seven dollars and fifty cents in total.

B: Here you go.

A: Out of fifty. _____ _____ _____. Have a good
day.

◇関連表現◇   上記の下線の文と併せて覚えましょう。

    1   この手紙を日本に航空便でお願いします。

      I want to send this letter to Japan by airmail.

    2   この手紙の郵送代はいくらですか。

      How much postage do I need for this letter?

One Step Forward 6

次の省略語の意味は何でしょう。日本語発音だと［v］と［b］の区別が無く、
後者になりかねません。

TV と TB
I have a TV. を I have a TB. と発音すると周りはどう反応するか・・・。

答 ☞ 次頁。

One Step Forward 6 の答

TV は television（テレビ）の略で、TB は tuberculosis（結核 ＊伝染性が強い）の略。

Unit 7　Literal Translation

Ⅰ　Vocabulary Checking

A群の英単語の日本語訳をB群より選びその記号を〔　　〕に記入しなさい。

A群

　1 capital 　　〔　　〕　　2 promise 　　〔　　〕　　3 emergency 　　〔　　〕

　4 translation 〔　　〕　　5 signature 〔　　〕　　6 comfortable 〔　　〕

B群

　a 署名　　**b** 翻訳　　**c** 緊急　　**d** 快適な、リラックスした　　**e** 首都　　**f** 約束

Ⅱ　Reading

CD 1-26

☆ **Before Reading Passage** (Q〔質問〕を念頭に passage〔本文〕を読んでみましょう)

　Q1 約束にあたる英単語　promise と appointment の違いは？

　Q2「首都は何処」「この席空いてますか」「サインを下さい」「危ない！」「アンケートに答えて」の英語訳は？

☆ **Words & Phrases** (単語、語句のヒント)

　1 literal translations 文字通り訳　　2 awkward ぎこちない　　3 likewise 同様に

　4 celebrities 有名人　　5 handwriting 手書き　　6 document 文書

　7 hang out ぶらぶらする　　8 fill in 記入する、答える

☆ **Passage**

　In learning a foreign language, [1]literal translations often result in [2]awkward expressions. Suppose you are arranging to meet Mr. Smith. You usually decide when and where to meet him. Never say, "When are you convenient?" but say "When is it convenient for you?" Then you may say "I have a promise to see Mr. Smith." It should be "I have an appointment to see Mr. Smith." 'Promise' means to say that you will do something.

　If you find an empty seat on a train, you may ask the person sitting next to the seat, "Is this seat empty?" You do not need to ask because you can easily tell that no one is sitting there. Just say "Is this seat taken?" or "Are you saving this seat for someone?" Also, if you want to know the capital of the U.S., just say, "What is the capital of the U.S.?" If you say, "Where is the capital of the U.S.?", it is a question to ask the location of the capital on a map or the way to get there. [3]Likewise, rather than asking, "Which number should I call in case of an emergency?" it is better to ask, "What number should I call in case of an emergency?"

If you want an autograph from some foreign [4]celebrities such as TV stars and famous writers or athletes, just say, "Could I have your autograph? Never say "Could you sign, please?" or "Can I have your sign?" Use the word autograph, which means a famous person's name written in his or her own [5]handwriting. The word **sign** means to write your name on a letter or [6]document to show that you wrote it or agree with it. You may be asked for your signature when shopping or paying by credit card.

When you can hardly hear your teacher in the class, you may ask him or her to speak louder, not in a bigger voice. When you have a guest at home and want him or her to relax, say "Please make yourself comfortable." instead of saying "Please relax." Also, just say "Watch out!" for "It is dangerous!" Likewise, it is better to say to [7]**hang out with friends** instead of saying 'to go play with your friends'. At the end of the semester, your teacher may ask you some questions about the classes. Just say, "[8]Fill in the questionnaire." Never say "Answer the *ankēto*" , which does not make sense in English at all.

III Listening Comprehension

Listen to the CD and choose the correct answer about the passage.

1   A   to decide where and when to meet someone

   B   to say that you will surely do something

   C   It means the same as the word **appointment**.

2   A   You are asking the name of the U.S. capital.

   B   It is Washington D.C.

   C   You are asking the capital's location on a map.

3   A   when you shop and pay by a card

   B   Some TV stars may be asked by their fans.

   C   Yes, the word signature is sometimes used for the word **sign**.

4   A   They may ask you to fill in the questionnaire.

   B   to speak louder

   C   They may tell you to go and hang out with your friends after the class.

Additional Listening Practice 7

Listen to the CD and choose the best answer or a statement as a response

1   A   B   C

2   A   B   C

Ⅳ　Writing Exercise 7（完了形）

Exercise 1　［　　］内の語（句）を並べ替え日本文にあう英文を書いてみましょう。

（注：文頭の文字サイズと句読点は、要適宜対応）

　1　僕は、まだ宿題を終えていない。

[have, yet, homework, not, I, my, finished]

→_____

　2　春が来たけど、まだ寒いです。

［still, is, come, spring, cold, has, it, but]

→_____

　3　私の祖母は、先週から病気で寝ています。

[been, since, in bed, last, has, sick, week, my grandma]

→_____

Exercise 2　次の各日本文にあう英文を書いてみましょう。

　1　その男の子は今朝、起きてから何も食べていない。

→_____

_____

　2　「ニューヨークに住んでどれくらいになりますか。」「こちらに住んで3年になります。」

→_____

_____

　3　トムとトモ子は2010年にニューヨークの大学で会って以来の知り合いです。

→_____

_____

Ⅴ　Dialog（ミニ英会話 7）

Listen to the CD and fill in the blanks.（CD を聴き空白部分を書き取りましょう）

At a Gift Shop（土産店で）　[A: A store clerk　B: A female customer]

A: Good afternoon. May I help you?

B: Yes. I'm ＿＿＿＿＿＿＿ ＿＿＿＿＿＿＿ ＿＿＿＿＿＿＿
＿＿＿＿＿＿＿ for my mother.

A: What kind of gift ＿＿＿＿＿＿＿ ＿＿＿＿＿＿＿ ＿＿＿＿＿＿＿
＿＿＿＿＿＿＿ ＿＿＿＿＿＿＿ ?

B: I have no idea. What do you recommend?

A: How about some perfume?

B: ＿＿＿＿＿＿＿ ＿＿＿＿＿＿＿ . It smells nice. How much is it?

A: $45, plus tax.

B: Fine. ＿＿＿＿＿＿＿ ＿＿＿＿＿＿＿ ＿＿＿＿＿＿＿ . Here's 50 dollars.

A: I'll be right back with your change.

◇関連表現◇　上記の下線の文と併せて覚えましょう。

1　それを贈り物用に包装してください。

Please gift-wrap it. ／ Will you have it gift-wrapped?

2　少し安くなりませんか。

Will you give me a discount?

3　「それを試着してもいいですか。」「勿論。あちらに試着室があります。」

"May / Can I try it on?"　"Sure. There's a fitting room over there."

One Step Forward 7

「私は黒い目をしている。」の正しい英訳はどちらでしょうか。

ア　I have black eyes.
イ　I have dark brown eyes.

答 ☞ 次頁。

One Step Forward 7 の答

イ　アは、「誰かに殴られたりして（目の）周りが黒く腫れ上がっている。」の意味。

Unit 8　An American Student on a Homestay Program ①

I　Vocabulary Checking

A群の英単語の日本語訳をB群より選びその記号を［　　］に記入しなさい。

A群

1 correct　［　］　　2 polish　　［　］　　3 weight　　［　］

4 container　［　］　　5 electricity　［　］　　6 consent　　［　］

B群

a 正しい　　**b** 電気　　**c** 体重、重さ　　**d** 容器　　**e** 同意（する）　　**f** 〜を磨く

II　Reading

CD
2-1

☆ **Before Reading Passage** （Q［質問］を念頭に passage［本文］を読んでみましょう）

Q1 アメリカの留学生をホームステイさせる際に準備しておきたい事項の一つに何がありますか？

Q2 日本語のホットケーキ、レンジ、リモコン、トイレ、コンセント、ノートパソコン等は正しい英語表現ですか？

☆ **Words & Phrases** （単語、語句のヒント）

1 edible 食用の　　　　　2 abbreviate 短縮する　　3 get rid of 〜を除く

4 refers to 〜のことを言う　5 permission 許可　　　　6 lower back 腰

7 producer メーカー、会社　8 locate 位置する、ある

☆ **Passage**

You may have a chance to have an American student on a homestay program at your place. Learning how to use correct English in daily life can be helpful for smooth communication with each other.

First, for food, you may serve the student a pancake, not a **hotto kēki** （hot cake） at breakfast. The student may like weak coffee, not **American coffee**, which is incorrect English. If the student likes sweets, he or she may enjoy a cream puff with lemon tea. For cream puff, many Japanese say **shūkurīmu** （shoe cream） which sounds like a cream to polish shoes and is not [1]edible at all. He or she may want some French Fries, not **furaido poteto** （fried potato） and a Coke, not **kōra** （cola）. Many people always watch their weight. A bathroom scale, not a **herusu mēta** （health meter）, will help them watch their weight.

Use the phrase plastic bottle for **petto botoru** (pet bottle), and frying pan for **fry pan**. Say microwave, not **renji**, to warm up food, but never say **chin**, which means the part of the jaw below the mouth.

Avoid shortened or [2]abbreviated forms of English as much as possible. Use either ice cube or ice cream to make it clear what you mean by **ice**. Use commercials instead of **CM**, air conditioner for an **eakon**, and remote control for **rimokon**. Do not say cooler for an air conditioner. A cooler means a container in which you can keep food or drinks cool. Also, avoid the word **toire** and toilet but say washroom, bathroom or restroom instead. Toilet means a large bowl on which you sit to [3]get rid of waste out of your body. A similar word lavatory usually [4]refers to a small room in a plane or a train.

In her room, the American student may use a laptop computer, not **nōto pasokon** and an electric carpet, not **hot carpet**. Use the word outlet for the **konsento**, a place in a wall to connect electrical devices to the electricity supply. The similar sound English word consent means [5]permission or agreement to do something. "We need your parent's written **consent** before you have an operation on your [6]lower back." Also, the word **outlet** has another meaning of a store selling the goods of a particular [7]producer at a discount price, but not necessarily [8]located in the suburbs as one in Japan, though.

Ⅲ Listening Comprehension

CD
2-2

Listen to the CD and choose the correct answer about the passage.

1   A   a bathroom scale

    B   Yes, people always watch how much they weigh.

    C   sweets such as cream puffs

2   A   Say iced cream instead of saying ice cream.

    B   It is unclear whether it means ice cream or ice cube.

    C   It means ice cream in most cases.

3   A   in a bathroom

    B   in an airplane

    C   Yes, you can find a toilet in the lavatory.

4   A   permission or agreement to do something

    B   a place in a wall to connect electrical devices to the electricity supply

    C   a store selling the goods of a particular maker at a low price

Additional Listening Practice 8

Listen to the CD and choose the best answers to the questions.

1 A He lost his wallet.

   B He missed the bus to the bus terminal near the hotel.

   C He doesn't know where he is.

   D He has to get back to the hotel in five minutes.

2 A He will walk to the hotel.

   B He will take a taxi to get to the hotel.

   C He will ask another person the way to the hotel.

   D He will walk to the nearest bus stop.

IV Writing Exercise 8 （不定詞）

Exercise 1 ［　　］内の語（句）を並べ替え日本文にあう英文を書いてみましょう。

(注：文頭の文字サイズと句読点は、要適宜対応)

1 その小さな女の子は、その大きな犬を見て泣き出した。

[she, cry, saw, to, when, began, dog, the little, the big, girl]

→＿＿＿＿＿＿＿＿＿＿＿＿＿＿＿＿＿＿＿＿＿＿

2 この英語の本を読むのは我々には非常に難しい。

[for, is, it, this, read, hard, us, English, to, very, book]

→＿＿＿＿＿＿＿＿＿＿＿＿＿＿＿＿＿＿＿＿＿＿

3 新しい CD を我々と一緒に聴きませんか（聴きたいですか）。

[new, to, want, listen, with, you, do, the, us, to, CD]

→＿＿＿＿＿＿＿＿＿＿＿＿＿＿＿＿＿＿＿＿＿＿

Exercise 2 次の各日本文にあう英文を書いてみましょう。

1 兄は僕に机の上の彼のパソコンに触れないように言った。

→＿＿＿＿＿＿＿＿＿＿＿＿＿＿＿＿＿＿＿＿＿＿

＿＿＿＿＿＿＿＿＿＿＿＿＿＿＿＿＿＿＿＿＿＿

2 この大きな箱は重すぎて僕には運べない。それを運ぶには、誰か手伝ってくれる者が必要だ。

→＿＿＿＿＿＿＿＿＿＿＿＿＿＿＿＿＿＿＿＿＿＿

＿＿＿＿＿＿＿＿＿＿＿＿＿＿＿＿＿＿＿＿＿＿

（次頁に続く）

3　父は退職後にアメリカ一周旅行をしてみたいと言っている。

[ヒント：退職する ☞ retire、一周 ☞ around]

→ _____

_____

_____

V　Dialog（ミニ英会話 8）

CD
2-4

Listen to the CD and fill in the blanks.（CD を聴き空白部分を書き取りましょう）

Checking in at the Airport（空港でのチェックイン）　[A: An airline staff member

B: A passenger]

A: Hi! May I help you?

B: Yes. _____ _____ _____

_____ _____.

A: All right. _____ _____ _____

_____, please.

B: Here they are.

A: _____ _____ _____

_____ _____ _____?

B: Two. But I want to keep this small bag with me.

A: Fine. Window seat or aisle seat?

B: Window seat, please. Is _____ _____

_____ _____?

A: Yes, it is. Okay. All set. Here's your boarding pass.

_____ _____ _____ _____.

◇関連表現◇　上記の下線の文と併せて覚えましょう

1　我々二人、隣どうしの席をお願いできますか。

Can we have seats next to each other?

2　「何か飲み物はいかがですか。」「赤ワインを一杯ください。」

"Would you like something to drink?"　"A glass of red wine, please."

One Step Forward 8

How Do You Say it in English?　（次の日本語にあたる英単語（句）は何でしょう。）

① ショッピングバッグ　② キッチンタオル　③　サランラップ　④　タッパー

答 ☞ 次頁。

One Step Forward 8 の答

① ショッピングバッグ　a plastic bag

② キッチンタオル　paper towel

③ サランラップ　plastic wrap

④ タッパー　a plastic container

Unit 9　An American Student on a Homestay Program ②

I　Vocabulary Checking

A群の英単語の日本語訳をB群より選びその記号を［　　］に記入しなさい。

A群

1 steer 　　［　　］　　2 experience 　［　　］　　3 unemployed ［　　］

4 discount 　［　　］　　5 prefix 　　　［　　］　　6 preferable 　［　　］

B群

a 経験　　**b** 割引(する)　　**c** 好ましい　　**d** 接頭語　　**e** ～を操作する　　**f** 失業した、無職の

II　Reading

CD
2-5

☆ **Before Reading Passage**（Q［質問］を念頭に passage［本文］を読んでみましょう）

Q1 留学生にバイキングレストラン、スーパー、ガソリンスタンド、ハンドル、タイムセール等は英語として通じますか?

Q2 留学生が日本で見聞きする英語の接頭語 're［リ]' のついた語の例にはどんな語がありますか。

☆ **Words & Phrases**（単語、語句のヒント）

1 proper 正しい　　　　　2 station attendants 店員　　　　　3 reduced 差し引いた

4 witness ～を見かける　　5 renovation 増改築　　　　　　6 pawn shop 質屋

7 article 記事　　　　　　8 restructuring 経営方針・組織等の改編

☆ **Passage**

You may help an American student experience a lot of things during his or her stay in Japan. You may take him or her for **Sushi** or **Yakiniku** at a restaurant. Never say, "Let's go to a *viking* restaurant," but say "Let's have dinner at an all-you-can-eat Sushi restaurant" or simply "Let's go to a buffet restaurant."

You may give the American student a ride for shopping at a supermarket, not a **sūpā** (super) or a grocery store or a mall. On the way, you may stop by at a *gasoline stand*. The phrase *gasoline stand*, however, is not [1]proper English and it should be a gas station or service station. The student may be surprised to learn that the [2]station attendants may offer to clean the windshield, not the **furonto garasu** (front glass), free of charge. He or she might be interested in sitting behind the wheel someday while staying in Japan. The Japanese word **handoru** (handle) in a car is called a steering wheel or simply a wheel in English and thus sitting or being behind the wheel means to drive a car. The noun **handle** in English means the part of a door or a window to open it. It also means the part of a tool, knife, or pot that you hold to use or carry it. At a store, the student may enjoy buying things at [3]reduced or discounted prices when they offer a limited-time sale not **taimu sēru** (time sale).

While staying in Japan, the American student may often [4]witness or hear Japanese using English words with the prefix 're'. While some words are correctly used, some others are not. The student may have some inconvenience if part of the house where he or she is staying is under [5]renovation, not **rifōmu** (reform). The student may be interested in shopping at a second hand shop or a [6]pawn shop, not a **risaikuru shoppu** (recycle shop). The student may hear the word in news or see an [7]article in a newspaper about *risutora*, a shortened form of the word [8]restructuring. It should be being laid-off or to get fired if it is meant to get unemployed.

The American student may love to wear a Japanese **kimono** while in Japan. He or she will be even more delighted to have one as a gift or a souvenir. To make him or her happier, a **custom-made** or **tailor-made** kimono, not an **ōdā meido** (order made) kimono, is preferable.

III   Listening Comprehension

Listen to the CD and choose the correct answer about the passage.

1   A   A tailor-made **kimono** may.

   B   Yes, shopping at a second hand store may.

   C   an article in a newspaper

2   A   They have the time-limited service there.

   B   A staff there may clean the windshield for free.

   C   Service station is another way to say it.

3   A   Yes, it is better to say 'behind the steering wheel'.

   B   It means to handle.

   C   to drive a car

4   A   in a house under renovation

   B   at a buffet restaurant

   C   at a store

Additional Listening Practice 9

Listen to the CD and choose the best answer or a statement as a response.

1   A   B   C

2   A   B   C

Ⅳ   Writing Exercise 9（比較①）

Exercise 1   [   ] 内の語（句）を並べ替え日本文にあう英文を書いてみましょう。

（注：文頭の文字サイズと句読点は、要適宜対応）

1   春と秋、どちらが好きですか。

[do, better, fall, which, you, spring, like, or]

→ _____

2   僕は君ほどお金を持ち合わせていない。

[money, as, I, have, you, much, don't, as]

→ _____

3   富士山が日本で一番高い山だということは誰もが知っている。

[is, knows, Japan, the, in, everybody, that, highest, Mt. Fuji, mountain]

→ _____

Exercise 2   次の各日本文にあう英文を書いてみましょう。

1   テイラー・スイフトは、今、アメリカで最も人気のある若手女性歌手の一人です。

→ _____

_____

2   彼は音楽制作者としてよりも、あるバンドの歌手としてよく知られていたようだ。

→ _____

_____

3   今朝の温度は昨日よりずっと低かった。実際、今朝はこの冬一番の寒さだった。

→ _____

_____

V　Dialog（ミニ英会話 9）

Listen to the CD and fill in the blanks.（CD を聴き空白部分を書き取りましょう）

Asking the Way（道を尋ねる）［A: A foreigner　B: A Japanese ］

A: Excuse me. _____ _____ _____

_____?

B: Yes, some. _____ _____ _____

_____?

A: Yes, where's the nearest post office?

B: It's the white building right across the street.

A: Oh, _____ _____ _____.

B: You are welcome.

◇関連表現◇　　上記の下線の文と併せて覚えましょう。

　　　　1　　この辺は私も不案内です。

　　　　　　I am a stranger here myself.

　　　　2　　すぐにわかりますよ。

　　　　　　You can't miss it.

One Step Forward 9

How Do You Say it in English?　（次の日本語にあたる英単語（句）は何でしょう。）

① ミキサー　　② ドアホン　　③ フローリング　　④ システムバス

答 ☞ 次頁。

One Step Forward 9 の答

① ミキサー　blender

② ドアホン　intercom

③ フローリング　wooden floor

④ システムバス　a modular bathroom

Unit 10　Sports

Ⅰ　Vocabulary Checking

A群の英単語の日本語訳をB群より選びその記号を ［　　］ に記入しなさい。

A群

1　domestic　［　　］　　　2　encourage　［　　］　　　3　athletes　［　　］

4　shorten　［　　］　　　5　fist　　　　［　　］　　　6　violence　［　　］

B群

a 国内の　　**b** 暴力　　**c** 拳　　**d** ～を励ます　　**e** 短縮する　　**f** スポーツ選手

Ⅱ　Reading

☆ **Before Reading Passage**（Q［質問］を念頭に passage［本文］を読んでみましょう）

Q1 スポーツ等でよく使う「ドンマイ」は英語なのでしょうか。

Q2 日本人の言うガッツポーズ、ハイタッチ、バトンバッチ、スキンシップ等の正しい英語表現は？

☆ **Words & Phrases**（単語、語句のヒント）

1 indoor arenas 屋内競技場　　2 manager（s）監督　　3 opponent（s）対戦相手　　4 appropriate 適切な

5 determination 決意　　　6 clenched 握りしめた　　7 crowds 観客　　　8 retire 退職する

☆ **Passage**

Many people get excited at players' performances at the time of the Olympic Games, the soccer World Cup, and other domestic or international sport games or events. Fans cheer on athletes in stadiums, ballparks, or ¹indoor arenas while many others do so while watching TV.

Players often cheer on each other, too. When a teammate or one of the pair did not play well or could have done better, in Japan, he or she might say, "**Don mai,**" a shortened phrase of "**Don't mind**", neither of which make sense to native English speakers. Use such expressions as 'Never mind.', 'No big deal' 'Don't worry about it' or 'Forget about it.'

Coaches or baseball ²managers usually encourage their players on the field or the court or send them there as they say something like, 'Go for it', 'Hang in there." "Do your best". In these cases, many Japanese often use **Fight!** which means to argue or attack the [3]opponents by violence and thus is not [4]appropriate except in boxing matches and so on. The word **fight** also means fighting spirit, though. Another incorrect English expression is **Gattsu pôzu** (guts pose) when a player scores or does a great play, or the team wins. The word **guts** means bravery or [5]determination to do or say something. "Tom did not have the guts to say what he really thought." For a nice play or scoring, just say, "They raised their [6]clenched fists to express their joy." The same holds true when the team wins. Also, some players at the bench as well as the [7]crowds in the stands may exchange **hai tacchi** (high touch) to each other to express their joy. **High-five** is natural English.

Similarly, another Japanese-English phrase **baton tacchi** (baton touch) does not make sense. Use such phrases as **baton pass** or to **pass the baton** or **changeover** in a relay race. Japanese also use the phrase to mean giving control of something such as a company to someone. Instead of saying, "Turning 70 years old this fall, I will **do baton-tacchi** my company to my son next spring," just say, "My son will **take over** the company next spring after I [8]retire this fall turning 70 years old."

Some coaches train the players in regular practices not by **sukin shippu** (skin ship) but by physical contact. If you are a baseball player, start warming up by playing catch, not by **kyacchi bōru** (catch ball).

III Listening Comprehension

CD
2-10

Listen to the CD and choose the correct answer about the passage.

1 A It makes no sense in English.

   B It means the same as "Don't worry about it."

   C It is used to cheer up your teammate.

2 A when his or her teammate scores

   B when his or her teammate could have done better

   C Yes, it is often used by a coach or a manager.

3 A to show their joy

   B the players at the bench as well as the crowds in the stands

   C when the team scores five points

4 A It is used to mean to take over a job.

   B It is one of the Japanese-English phrases.

   C It is an expression used in a relay race.

Additional Listening Practice 10

Listen to the CD and choose the best answers to the questions.

1 A two for her brothers   B three, two for her parents and one for herself

   C two for her parents   D two ties and some perfume for her parents

2 A They were reasonable.

   B They were very high and she bought only a tie.

   C They were too high, but she got a discount.

   D The gifts cost her 150 dollars in total.

Ⅳ Writing Exercise 10 （比較②）

Exercise 1 ［　　　］内の語（句）を並べ替え日本文にあう英文を書いてみましょう。

（注：文頭の文字サイズと句読点は、要適宜対応）

1 この新しい橋はその古い橋の２倍の幅がある。

［wide, new, is, one, twice, as, this, bridge, as, the old］

→ _____

2 春が来て、だんだん暖かくなっている。

［has, warmer, it, and, is, spring, warmer, come, and, getting］

→ _____

3 メアリーはクラスで他のどの生徒よりも多くの本を読みます。

［any, her, in, reads, student, more, class, than, Mary, other, books］

→ _____

Exercise 2 次の各日本文にあう英文を書いてみましょう。

1 娘は、テレビを見るより本を読むのが好きなようだ。

［ヒント：Ｂより Ａ を好む ☞ prefer A to B］

→ _____

_____

2 多くの人は、ロサンゼルスがアメリカで２番目に大きい都市であることを知らない。

→ _____

_____

3 現在、市役所近くに建設中のその新しい文化センターは旧文化センターの約３倍の大きさになる。

→ _____

_____

V Dialog（ミニ英会話 10）

Listen to the CD and fill in the blanks.（CD を聴き空白部分を書き取りましょう）

Taking the Subway to the Airport（空港へは地下鉄で）〔A: A foreigner　B: A Japanese〕

A: Excuse me. Do you speak English?

B: Yes, a little. _____ _____ _____ _____ _____?

A: How can I get to the airport?

B: Take the subway.

A: _____ _____ _____ _____ _____?

B: Two hundred and fifty yen, I think.

A: And_____ _____ _____ _____ _____?

B: About fifteen minutes.

A: Thank you so much.

B:_____ _____ _____.

◇関連表現◇　　上記の下線の文と併せて覚えましょう。

    1　片道ですか往復ですか。

      One way or round trip?

    2　乗り換えなければなりませんか。

      Do I have to change trains?

    3　何番ホームから出発しますか。

      Which platform/track does the train leave from?

One Step Forward 10

How Do You Say it in English?　　（次の日本語にあたる英単語（句）は何でしょう。）

① スタメン　　② デッドボール　　③ ホームベース

④ フライング（スタート）　　⑤ サンドバッグ

答 ☞ 次頁。

One Step Forward　10 の答

① スタメン　starting lineup

② デッドボール　hit by a pitch

③ ホームベース　the home plate

④ フライング（スタート）　false start

⑤ サンドバッグ　a punching bag

Unit 11　Free and Just

I　Vocabulary Checking

A群の英単語の日本語訳をB群より選びその記号を［　］に記入しなさい。

A群

1 cost 　　［　　］ 　　2 phrase 　［　　］ 　　3 valid 　［　　］

4 company 　［　　］ 　　5 express 　［　　］ 　　6 fee 　　［　　］

B群

a 会社 　　**b** 費用（がかかる） 　　**c** 表現する 　　**d** 有効な 　　**e** 料金 　　**f** 語句

II　Reading

CD
2-13

☆ **Before Reading Passage**（Q［質問］を念頭に passage［本文］を読んでみましょう）

Q1 日本人が使うフリーアナウンサーやフリータイム等は英語なのでしょうか。

Q2 ジャストタイムやジャストサイズはどうでしょうか。

☆ **Words & Phrases**（単語、語句のヒント）

1 noun 名詞 　　　2 restrict 制限する 　　　3 otherwise 別の言い方で 　　　4 purchase 購入する

5 likewise 同様に 　　6 misuse 誤用する

☆ **Passage**

One of the most widely but incorrectly used English words among Japanese is a phrase with such words as **free** and **just**, usually used before a [1]noun. Try to learn the correct usage of any foreign words for better communication.

The word **free** in English means; not being controlled or [2]restricted; costing no money; not busy. Japanese often use such words as **free announcer**, **free journalist** and **free cameraman**, to name a few. They all should be a freelance announcer, a freelance journalist, and a freelance photographer. On the other hand, the word free in "free time" should be expressed [3]otherwise. Some *karaoke* shops put up a sign, "Free time from 10 AM to 6 PM for ¥2000 per person." This should be expressed, "Flat fee ¥2000 per person: from 10 AM to 6 PM".

In another case, some Japanese say, "I [4]purchased a **free pass** for the theme park." This sounds quite strange because you do not buy a pass if it is free. You could say "I won a free pass for the theme park." You can also say, "I got two free tickets for the concert." As for the pass, just say 'one-day pass.' if it is valid for a day. [5]Likewise, use the phrase **toll free** for **furī daiaru** (free dial) in making a free call. You may present someone very tall a large-size or **furī saizu** (free size) or **ōru saizu** (all size) T-shirt. The right English phrase here is **one-size-fits-all**.

Similarly, many Japanese often [6]misuse the word **just** in a phrase. The phrases such as **jyasuto fyitto** (just fit) and **jyasuto saizu** (just size) are good examples. The phrase **just fit** should be to 'fit perfectly' or to 'fit quite well.' "I love the new suit. It fits me quite well! Or "This just fits!" Also, use the phrase **perfect size** or **correct size** for **jyasuto saizu**. Likewise, if you say 'It's **just** nine o'clock', it not only means **exactly** nine o'clock but also **only** nine o'clock and not being so late. "I've got to get going." "Oh, you've got to? It's just nine o'clock." "It happened just a few weeks ago", means that several weeks is not a long period of time.

III Listening Comprehension

CD
2-14

Listen to the CD and choose the correct answer about the passage.

1   A   a freelance journalist
    B   a free dial
    C   perfect size

2   A   a free call
    B   It means a free pass for a concert.
    C   a large-size shirt for someone tall

3   A   Nothing is wrong with it.
    B   You can win a free pass for it.
    C   You do not pay any money for a pass if it is free.

4   A   When it is getting quite late at night.
    B   When it is a few minutes before nine o'clock.
    C   When it is only nine o'clock and not so late yet.

Additional Listening Practice 11

CD
2-15

Listen to the CD and choose the best answer or a statement as a response.

1   A   B   C
2   A   B   C

Ⅳ Writing Exercise 11（関係代名詞）

Exercise 1 ［　　］内の語（句）を並べ替え日本文にあう英文を書いてみましょう。

（注：文頭の文字サイズと句読点は、要適宜対応）

1 私には母が有名なピアニストの友人がいます。

[a famous, is, whose, a friend, have, pianist, I, mother]

→ _____

2 父が先月買った新車は、とても燃費が良い。

[is, fuel-efficient, bought, the new car, my father, very, which, last month]

→ _____

3 君はあそこで私の母と話している男性を知っていますか。

[the man, is, with, there, do, my mother, know, you, over, who, talking]

→ _____

Exercise 2 次の各日本文にあう英文を書いてみましょう。

1 先々週、君が買った新しいパソコンを私達に見せてください。

［ヒント：先々週 ☞ 先週の前の週］

→ _____

_____

2 ホワイト氏は、その村の全員がとても尊敬している医師です。

→ _____

_____

3 多くの人は、よく嘘をつくボブを信頼していない。しかし、今朝、彼が言ったこと
は本当だと思う。

→ _____

_____

V Dialog （ミニ英会話 11）

Listen to the CD and fill in the blanks.（CD を聴き空白部分を書き取りましょう）

Asking Questions 1　（質問をする）［A: A Japanese learning English　B: An American］

A: May I ask you a question?

B: _____.　_____　_____　_____.

A: _____　_____　_____　_____

　　"**PETTO BOTORU**" in English?

B: We say "plastic bottle."

A: Thanks a lot.

B:_____　_____　_____.

◇関連表現◇　上記の下線の文と併せて覚えましょう。

　　　1　この単語はどう発音するのですか。

　　　　How do you pronounce this word?

　　　2　その単語 / 君の名前　のつづりは？

　　　　How do you spell the word / your name?

One Step Forward 11

フリー (free) やジャスト (just) と同様に日本語でもよく使う「ミス (間違い、間違う)」は、たぶんに英語の 'mistake' の頭の部分に由来しているようです。では日本語の同音の英単語 'miss' はどういう意味でしょうか。以下の英文の意味を考えてみましょう。

① I missed you. (≒ I love you.) ／ I miss living in the city.
② I missed you at lunch yesterday. (＝ I didn't see you at lunch time yesterday.)
③ We missed the beginning of the movie.
④ Tom often finds an error that everyone else usually misses.
⑤ I didn't miss my key until I got home.

答 ☞ 次頁。

One Step Forward 11 の答

① I missed you. (≒ I love you.) / I miss living in the city.

君に会いたかった。 / 都会生活が懐かしい。

② I missed you at lunch yesterday. (＝ I didn't see you at lunch time yesterday.)

昨日、お昼時、見かけなかったね。

③ We missed the beginning of the movie.

我々は映画の最初の部分を見損なった。

④ Tom often finds an error that everyone else usually misses.

トムは他の人が普通見落とす間違いによく気づく。

⑤ I didn't miss my key until I got home.

帰宅して鍵が無いのに気づいた。

Unit 12 My Car

I Vocabulary Checking

A群の英単語の日本語訳をB群より選びその記号を［　　］に記入しなさい。

A群

1 recent　　［　　］　　2 government ［　　］　　3 original　［　　］

4 confusion ［　　］　　5 expression　［　　］　　6 sentence ［　　］

B群

a 独自の、元の　　**b** 最近の　　**c** 表現　　**d** 政府　　**e** 文章　　**f** 混乱

II Reading

☆ **Before Reading Passage**（Q［質問］を念頭に passage［本文］を読んでみましょう）

Q1 日本語では「マイカー」「マイホーム」等「マイ〜」という表現を見かけます。正しい英語表現でしょうか？

Q2 my car を使った英文例の問題点は？ my bag、my number はそれぞれの正しい使い方を読みとりましょう。

☆ **Words & Phrases**（単語、語句のヒント）

1 coin 造語する　　　　　　　2 seed 種　　　　　　　　3 native English speakers 英語母語者

4 global warming 地球温暖化　　5 reduce 〜を削減する　　6 emission 排出

7 carbon dioxide 二酸化炭素　　8 bureaucracy 官庁、政府

☆ **Passage**

Japanese people seem to be quite good at ¹coining their own original English expressions. However, this so-called Japanese-English can often be a ²seed of confusion and misunderstanding in communication with ³native English speakers. The use of **my such-and-such** is a good example. People in Japan frequently use English expressions such as **my car**, **my home**, **my cup**, **my bag**, **my pace**, **my number**, and so on.

There is nothing wrong with these expressions when used correctly. In the case where the speaker is talking about their own car, for example, this is fine. If, however, the speaker were talking about someone else's car, this would be incorrect. Here is an example. "Do you have **my car**?" In Japanese English, the speaker probably means, "Do you have your own car?" If a native English speaker hears the question, they will understand it to mean that the speaker (A) is asking if the other person (B) has A's car. B seems to wonder if B has taken A's car. The correct question is, "Do you have your own car?" The same can be said about any Japanese English expression using **my**⋯ . Here is another example. "My grandma is highly conscious of [4]global warming. She thinks it quite important for each one of us to do what we can to [5]reduce [6]emissions of [7]carbon dioxide in our daily life. She always carries **my bag** when she shops at a grocery store." The last sentence should be, "She always carries **her own bag** when she shops at a grocery store."

The use of **my such-and-such** is so common in Japan, even the Japanese government has fallen into using it incorrectly. In Japan's [8]bureaucracy, the expression **My Number** is used in recent years. This is the official name of *kojin bangō*, which means **personal number**. Even though **My Number** is simple and easy to remember, it would be incorrect to ask someone, "Do you know My Number?" It would also be strange to ask, "Do you know your **My Number**?" It seems we may be stuck with this expression.

III Listening Comprehension

Listen to the CD and choose the correct answer about the passage.

1   A   Do you have my own car?

   B   It was not a long time ago when personal number came to be used in Japan.

   C   We had better not say, "Do you know your My Number?"

2   A   She worries about global warming.

   B   She asks strange questions about My Number.

   C   She carries her own bag in shopping for food.

3   A   in recent years

   B   It is not clear from the passage.

   C   Because it is easy and simple to remember.

4   A   Someone else has stolen the speaker's car.

   B   Do you have your own car?

   C   Yes, some native English speakers often hear the question.

Additional Listening Practice 12

Listen to the CD and choose the best answers to the questions.

1　A　two bags　　　B　one bag

　　C　three bags　　D　not clearly mentioned in the conversation

2　A　an aisle seat　　B　He wanted a window seat, but ended up with an aisle seat.

　　C　a window seat　D　The passenger said "Either will do."

Ⅳ　Writing Exercise 12 （形容詞 & 副詞）

Exercise 1　[　　]内の語（句）を並べ替え日本文にあう英文を書いてみましょう。

（注：文頭の文字サイズと句読点は、要適宜対応）

1　姉は彼女の新しい車を非常に慎重に乗ります。

[new, drives, sister, carefully, car, my, very, her]

→ _____

2　昨夜はとても暑かったので、我々はほとんど眠れなかった。

[hot, we, sleep, so, it, that, could, last, hardly, was, night]

→ _____

3　トムは一生懸命勉強したのでその難しい試験に合格できた。

[pass, because, hard, he, exam, could, very, the difficult, studied, Tom]

→ _____

Exercise 2　次の各日本文にあう英文を書いてみましょう。

1　僕は朝早く、空に奇妙な物を見た。

→ _____

_____

2　その講演はとてもつまらなくて私は途中で眠ってしまった。

[ヒント： つまらない ☞ boring]

→ _____

_____

3　今夜は早く寝なさい（寝た方が良い）。そうしないと明朝、バスに乗り遅れるよ。

[ヒント： そうしないと ☞ otherwise]

→ _____

_____

V Dialog（ミニ英会話 12）

Listen to the CD and fill in the blanks.（CD を聴き空白部分を書き取りましょう）

Asking Questions 2　[A: A Japanese student learning English　B: An American teacher]

A: ＿＿＿＿＿＿＿＿ ＿＿＿＿＿＿＿ ＿＿＿＿＿＿＿ ＿＿＿＿＿＿＿

＿＿＿＿＿＿＿ ＿＿＿＿＿＿＿?

B: Sure. ＿＿＿＿＿＿＿ ＿＿＿＿＿＿＿.

A: What does FYI stand for?

B: It stands for "For your information."

A: ＿＿＿＿＿＿＿ ＿＿＿＿＿＿＿?

B: It means "For your information."

A: I see. Thank you so much.

B: ＿＿＿＿＿＿＿.

◇関連表現◇　上記の下線の文と併せて覚えましょう。

1　どうもありがとうございます。　お安い御用です。/　朝飯前です。

　"Thanks a lot." "No sweat." "A piece of cake."

2　もう一度おっしゃってもらえますか。/　えっ、何とおっしゃいましたか。

　Will you say that again? / Excuse me?

One Step Forward 12

How Do You Say it in English?　　（次の日本語にあたる英単語（句）は何でしょう。）

① ノーメーク　　② マニキュア　　③ ヘアバンド、カチューシャ

④ ピアス

答 ☞ 次頁。

One Step Forward 12 の答

① ノーメーク wearing no make-up

② マニキュア nail polish

③ ヘアバンド、カチューシャ headband

④ ピアス earrings

注：英単語の pierce は「（耳等に）穴をあける」の意味でアクセサリーの意味はない

Unit 13　See, Look, and Watch

Ⅰ　Vocabulary Checking

A群の英単語の日本語訳をB群より選びその記号を［　　］に記入しなさい。

A群

　　1 whale　　［　］　　2 squirrel　［　］　　3 mistake　［　］

　　4 celebrate　［　］　　5 purpose　［　］　　6 drawing　［　］

B群

　　a 間違い　　**b** 絵画、絵を描くこと　　**c** 鯨　　**d** りす　　**e** 目的　　**f** 祝う

Ⅱ　Reading

☆ **Before Reading Passage** （Q［質問］を念頭に passage［本文］を読んでみましょう）

　Q1 英語の基本単語 see, look, watch にはどんな違いがあるのでしょうか。

　Q2「〜が見える」「ちょっと見て」「テレビ番組を見る」の「見る」にあたる英単語は？

☆ **Words & Phrases** （単語、語句のヒント）

　　1 encounter 出くわす　　2 usage 語法　　3 verb 動詞　　4 awesome 素晴らしい

　　5 effort 努力　　6 concentration 集中力　　7 similar 似た　　8 behave（行儀よく）振る舞う

☆ **Passage**

　Some English learners in Japan sometimes [1]encounter English words that are really confusing in their [2]usage. One typical example is three English [3]verbs **see**, **look**, and **watch**. These words are used when talking about using our eyes. You may easily make mistakes with these words, but fortunately, the listener will most likely understand what you mean. Here are some useful tips to use these words correctly.

　The word **see** is a general word about sight. "I can see the squirrel up in the tree. Can you see it?" We saw some whales last weekend from the ferry. It was [4]awesome to see them." "Have you ever seen a ghost?" "I see it, but I don't believe it." So, the image of something comes into your eyes, and you can see it. Of course, if the image does not come into your eyes, you can't see it. "I can't see anything! Please turn on the light."

　The word **look** is more specific than **see**. When we look, or look at something, we do it with purpose. We try to do it. We make some [5]effort, even if it is a small effort. "Look at me! I can ride a bicycle!" "I am looking at that tree, but I can't see the squirrel." What are you looking at? Are you looking at the strange cloud?" "Look!" It's a bird. It's a plane. No, it's Superman!" "Please take a look at my drawing. What do you think?" So, with some [6]concentration, we look or look at things. If you don't want to see something, don't look at it.

The word **watch** is [7]similar to **look**, but it is used when using more effort to see something. When we watch something or someone, we expect something to happen. The thing we are watching is going to change in some way. "What are you watching?" "Have you been watching that great drama series on TV?" "Lots of people watched the ball drop in Times Square to celebrate the New Year." "Hey, kids. I'm watching you. [8]Behave yourselves."

You will certainly make errors in using these words when speaking to others in English. Like any skill, with practice, you will improve over time.

III Listening Comprehension

Listen to the CD and choose the correct answer about the passage.

1 A in the ocean from a ferry
   B in a tree
   C when we turn on the light

2 A a celebration of the New Year
   B There is a big clock telling time there in New York.
   C great drama series on TV

3 A People watch someone or something expecting something to happen.
   B You need some concentration when you look at things.
   C The word look is quite different from the word watch.

4 A The listener may get angry.
   B The listener probably understands the speaker.
   C The speaker has just started learning English.

Listen to the CD and choose the best answer or a statement as a response.

1　A　B　C

2　A　B　C

Ⅳ　Writing Exercise 13（分詞 & 動名詞）

Exercise 1　[　　]内の語（句）を並べ替え日本文にあう英文を書いてみましょう。

（注：文頭の文字サイズと句読点は、要適宜対応）

1　僕は、英語で書かれたそのメールが理解できなかった。

[in, not, I, written, understand, English, could, the e-mail]

➜_____

2　間違いをするのを恐れてはいけません。

[of, making, be, mistakes, afraid, don't]

➜_____

3　彼は目を閉じたままで、その部屋の中をしばらく歩いた。

[with, while, eyes, he, for, the room, walked, in, a, his, closed]

➜_____

Exercise 2　次の各日本文にあう英文を書いてみましょう。

1　父は健康のために酒もタバコも止めた。（酒を飲むことと煙草を吸うこと）

➜_____

_____

2　あの老人に以前、何処かで会ったと思う（ことを憶えている）。

➜_____

_____

3　待合室はとても騒がしかったので、弟は名前が呼ばれたのに気付か（聞こえ）なかった。

［ヒント：待合室 ☞ a waiting room］

➜_____

_____

Listen to the CD and fill in the blanks. (CD を聴き空白部分を書き取りましょう)

Telephone 1 ［A: A Japanese office worker at a firm　B:Mr. White ］

A: Oriental Tech. May I help you?

B: Yes. This is Bob White at ABC Systems.

_____ _____ _____ _____

Mr. Saito in the Sales Department?

A: _____ _____, _____. I'm sorry, Mr. White.

But Mr. Saito is in a meeting right now. May I take a message?

B: Yes, please have him call me back sometime this afternoon.

_____ _____ _____ _____

_____.

A: Certainly. _____ _____ _____

_____ _____, Mr. White.

B: I appreciate it. Good bye.

A: Good bye.

◇関連表現◇　上記の下線の文と併せて覚えましょう。

1　今、彼は席をはずしています / 留守です / 外出中です。

He is not in right now.

2　どちら様でしょうか。

May I ask who is calling, please?

3　念のために電話番号をお願いします。

May I have your number just in case?

One Step Forward 13

How Do You Say it in English?　（次の日本語にあたる英単語（句）は何でしょう。）

① アルバイト　　② コンビニ　　③ サインペン

④ タッチパネル　　⑤ マスコミ

答☞ 次頁。

One Step Forward 13 の答

① アルバイト　a part time job

② コンビニ　a convenience store

③ サインペン　a felt pen

④ タッチパネル　a touch screen

⑤ マスコミ　mass media

I　Vocabulary Checking

A群の英単語の日本語訳をB群より選びその記号を［　］に記入しなさい。

A群

1　creator（s）［　］　　　2　term（s）［　］　　　3　edit　　　［　］

4　vocabulary　［　］　　　5　respond　［　］　　　6　destroy［　］

B群

a 創造者　　**b** 言葉、言い回し　　**c** 〜を破壊する　　**d** 応える　　**e** 語彙　　**f** 編集する

II　Reading

☆ **Before Reading Passage**（Q［質問］を念頭に passage［本文］を読んでみましょう）

Q1 ワンチャンとノウチャンの意味は？

Q2 学生生活で使用する「リュック」は英語？「ノート」は英語と同義？「さぼる（サボル）」の語源は？

☆ **Words & Phrases**（単語、語句のヒント）

1 guy 少年（男女含め若者の意あり）　　2 connection 関係　　3 absolutely 完全に

4 outdated 時代遅れの　　　　　　　　5 occur 発生する、起こる　　6 derive 由来する

7 neglect 〜を怠ける　　　　　　　　　8 updated 最新の

☆ **Passage**

Young people use a lot of Japanese English and may be the creators of new expressions. When a couple ¹guys see a girl they like, one of them might say to the other, "Wanchan." The other might respond, "Nochan." What they are talking about is the "one chance" he has in meeting her, talking with her, and getting to know her well. The response is "No chance," meaning he thinks there is no possibility of making a good ²connection with her. In proper English, one of the guys might say, "I think you have a chance with her." The other would respond, "I have no chance of that." They are nice, convenient expressions, but they are ³absolutely Japanese English.

A lot of classroom items are referred to in Japanese English, too. Some examples are **apuri** meaning application, **sumaho** meaning smartphone, **shāpupen** (taken from a product name) meaning mechanical pencil, and **hocchikisu** (a brand name) meaning stapler. Another example is **ryukku** meaning rucksack, which is now an [4]outdated term for a backpack or a book bag. Also, **purinto** (print) meaning a handout and **nōto** (note) meaning notebook are commonly used in class. However, a **nōto** (note) is, in fact, a short message, not a bound notebook. You can see where confusion can [5]occur when speaking to native English speakers using these terms.

There are other common expressions used by students as well as other people in Japan. These include **purikura** meaning print club. Print club could be described as a photo booth with photo editing features. Some college students often use the expression **saboru**, [6]deriving from **sabotage**. The word **sabotage** is from French but is used in English now. Japanese seem to use it to mean to skip class or even to skip work or [7]neglect work while on duty. In fact, the word in English or French usually means to damage or destroy something to harm an enemy.

See to it to learn and use [8]updated but proper English vocabulary and expressions as well as correct pronunciation. It will surely be helpful for better communication with native and other English speakers.

III Listening Comprehension

CD
2-26

Listen to the CD and choose the correct answer about the passage.

1 A as a product name
  B in a photo booth
  C in classes

2 A It is a new term for book bag.
  B It is taken from a brand name.
  C It is now better to say backpack instead of rucksack.

3 A either from English or Japanese
  B from French
  C to destroy something

4 A *Saboru* is used to mean skip class among Japanese.
  B The word note in English means both a notebook and a short message.
  C *Wanchan* and *nochan* may be convenient expressions.

Additional Listening Practice 14

Listen to two short conversations and choose the best answers to the questions.

1   A   It is quite old.   B   It was broken.

     C   It was set at forty degrees.   D   Nothing was wrong with it.

2   A   small car   B   renting a car

     C   a long sedan   D   for three days

Ⅳ　Writing Exercise 14 （前置詞）

Exercise 1 ［　　］内の語（句）を並べ替え日本文にあう英文を書いてみましょう。

（注：文頭の文字サイズと句読点は、要適宜対応）

1   私は、妹と一緒に自転車で通学します。

［go, my sister, by, school, with, to, bicycle, I］

→ _____

2   父は日曜日、普通在宅しています。

［at, Sundays, is, my father, home, usually, on］

→ _____

3   次の角で右に曲がり、そして川に沿って2ブロック歩いて行って下さい。

［along, the next, walk, for, right, two, at, corner, and, turn, the river, blocks］

→ _____

Exercise 2 次の各日本文にあう英文を書いてみましょう。

1   僕は英語の宿題を日曜日までに終えなければならない。

→ _____

_____

2   我々はコーヒーを飲みながらそのプロジェクトについて数時間話し合った。

［ヒント：飲みながら ☞ over］

→ _____

_____

3   玄関では靴を脱ぎ、そしてリビングではテーブルの上に足を置かないように。

→ _____

_____

V Dialog（ミニ英会話 14）

Listen to the CD and fill in the blanks.（CD を聴き空白部分を書き取りましょう）

Telephone 2 ［A: A foreigner　B: A Japanese］

A: Hello. ＿＿＿＿＿＿＿ ＿＿＿＿＿＿＿ ＿＿＿＿＿＿＿
＿＿＿＿＿＿＿ ＿＿＿＿＿＿＿, please?

B: Ken who?

A: Ken White, an American student staying with you this summer.

B: I'm afraid ＿＿＿＿＿＿＿ ＿＿＿＿＿＿＿ ＿＿＿＿＿＿＿
＿＿＿＿＿＿＿ ＿＿＿＿＿＿＿.

A: Oh, I'm sorry to have bothered you.

B: ＿＿＿＿＿＿＿ ＿＿＿＿＿＿＿.

◇関連表現◇　上記の下線の文と併せて覚えましょう。

　　　1　今、彼は別の電話に出ています。
　　　　　He is on another line.

　　　2　何か伝言はありますか。
　　　　　Would you like to leave a message?
　　　　　May I take a message?

One Step Forward 14

How Do You Say it in English?　（次の日本語にあたる英単語（句）は何でしょう。）

①　パーマ　　②　リンス　　③　プロポーション　　④　ベビーカー

答 ☞ 次頁。

One Step Forward 14 の答

① パーマ　a permanent wave or perm

② リンス　conditioner

③ プロポーション　figure

④ ベビーカー　stroller

Unit 15 Review +

I 次の1〜12のカタカナにあたる英単語(句)を下の枠内から選びなさい。

1 ガソリンスタンド   2 フリーダイアル   3 スリーサイズ

_____   _____   _____

4 ハンドル   5 フロントガラス   6 ヘルスメーター

_____   _____   _____

7 シュークリーム   8 ハイタッチ   9 ペットボトル

_____   _____   _____

10 サラリーマン / OL 11 スキンシップ   12 コンセント

_____   _____   _____

outlet   windshield   toll free (number)   plastic bottle   measurements cream puff   physical contact   bathroom scale   gas station   high-five steering wheel   office worker

II Choose a proper word or phrase in the (   ) in each sentence below.

以下の各文で（   ）内から適当な語（句）を選びなさい。

1 "Who are you looking for?" "I have (ア a promise   イ a reservation   ウ an appointment) to see Mr. Smith in the Sales Department.

2 It is right to say (ア free journalist   イ toll free   ウ free size) in English.

3 I want to buy a new (ア laptop   イ note personal   ウ desk-monitor) computer.

4 Sorry, we are (ア close   イ closing   ウ closed) today.

5 "Excuse me, but do you have (ア the time   イ time   ウ a watch)?" "Yes, it's just half past two."

6 "(ア Where   イ What   ウ Which) is the capital of Australia? Sydney?" "No. It's Canberra."

7 There are two different (ア spells   イ spellings   ウ spelling) for this word.

8 To ask a woman her (ア measurements   イ measures   ウ three size) is a very improper question.

9 Let me know when (ア it is convenient for you   イ are you convenient   ウ you are convenient) .

10 My elder sister wants to work at an airline company, not as a ground staff member, but as a (ア cabin attendant   イ stewardess   ウ flight attendant).

11 Being behind (ア the wheel   イ the handle   ウ the windshield) means to drive.

12 Please turn on the light. I can't (ア look   イ watch   ウ see) anything!

Answers

1	2	3	4	5	6
7	8	9	10	11	12

III Vocabulary Checking

Match the words and expressions with the definitions below.

次の英単語ア～タの意味を、下のA～Oから探しなさい。

ア promise [   ]   イ appointment   [   ]   ウ sign   [   ]   エ autograph [   ]

オ handle   [   ]   カ questionnaire [   ]   キ spell   [   ]   ク chip   [   ]

ケ measure [   ]   コ consent   [   ]   サ apart [   ]   シ depart   [   ]

ス guts   [   ]   セ cooler   [   ]   ソ major [   ]

A. a famous person's name written in his or her own writing

B. magic or a short period of time

C. the part of a door or a window to open it

D. to be separated by distance or time

E. bravery or determination to do or say something

F. permission or agreement to do something

G. to find the size, length or amount of something

H. the main subject you study at a college

I. a written set of questions about a subject given to a large number of people

J. to leave

K. a container in which you can keep food or drinks cool

L. to say that you will do something

M. a meeting that has been arranged for a particular time and place

N. a small piece of wood or stone, or a small piece of silicon used in computers

O. to write your name on a letter or document to show that you wrote it or agree with it

Ⅳ Writing Exercise 15 （it の用法）

Exercise 1 ［　　］内の語（句）を並べ替え日本文にあう英文を書いてみましょう。

（注：文頭の文字サイズと句読点は、要適宜対応）

1 次は僕の番です。

[is, my, next, turn, it]

→ _____

2 日本は今、秋で涼しくなっている。

[cool, Japan, is, in, now, it, fall, is, and, getting, it]

→ _____

3 その屋根の修理をするのに 10 万円かかった。

[to, the roof, me, 100,000 yen, fix, cost, it,]

→ _____

Exercise 2 次の各日本文にあう英文を書いてみましょう。

1 合意に至るのは難しいことが分かった。

[ヒント：分かる ☞ prove、合意 ☞ agreement]

→ _____

_____

2 暗くなってきたね。ここから今夜、我々が滞在するホテルまで距離はあとどれくらいあるの。

→ _____

_____

3 僕はその事故については、我々は何も言わないでおくのが良いと思う。

→ _____

_____

テキストの音声は、弊社 HP
http://www.eihosha.co.jp/の
「テキスト音声ダウンロード」
のバナーからダウンロードでき
ます。

Say It Right in English 2
ネイティブが気になる日本人の英語 2

2020年 1月15日　初　版

著　者© Mark Thompson
　　　　谷　岡　敏　博

発 行 者　佐　々　木　　元

発 行 所　株式会社 英　　宝　　社
〒 101-0032　東京都千代田区岩本町 2-7-7
☎ [03] (5833) 5870　Fax [03] (5833) 5872

ISBN 978-4-269-66049-6 C3582
印刷・製本：モリモト印刷株式会社

本書の一部または全部を、コピー、スキャン、デジタル化等での無
断複写・複製は、著作権法上での例外を除き禁じられています。本
書を代行業者等の第三者に依頼してのスキャンやデジタル化は、た
とえ個人や家庭内での利用であっても著作権侵害となり、著作権法
上一切認められておりません。